YOUR SAXON & VIKING

Homework Helper

by Alison Howard

How to use this book

Each topic in this book is clearly labelled and contains all these components:

Topic heading

Introduction to
the topic

Sub-topic 1 offers
complete information
about one aspect
of the topic

Choose a word
from the Keyword
Contents on page 3.
Then, turn to the
correct page and
look for your word
in **BOLD CAPITALS**.
This will take
you straight to
the information
you need

Viking Raids

**Words to use
in your project**

agrarian (agricultu...
assault (attack)
epic (an exciting st...

Vikings originated in the Scandinavian countries of Denmark, Sweden and Norway. Their countries were hilly, covered in forests and not always good for farming. As their population grew there was not enough land for everyone, so they were forced to carry out raids on neighbouring countries in northern Europe. Their boat-building and navigation skills meant that they soon started raiding the British Isles. They made swift ATTACKS on coastal areas, targeting monasteries, stealing treasures and capturing slaves.

SHIPS

Vikings had the advantage of fast ships, which they used to raid neighbouring countries.

Altho...
often...
and i...
also g...
The ...
mean...
to tra...
the m...
so Vi...
build...

The ...
for raiding...
and could be up to...
sails, but could also be r...
decorated with a frightening...
was protected with shields dow...
poem *Beowulf* describes the WEA...

*"They readied the ship on the waves under the cli...
prow as the water wound against the sand. The ...
bright weapons, fitted armour."*

An important Viking might be buried...
him and the possessions he would need...

Source – Beowulf, written down about 1000 AD

CAUSES OF RAIDS

After the Romans departed, it was not long before the Saxons started invading and settling. The native Britons had their own **TERRITORIES** which they fought hard to protect. As well as fighting the Britons, the Saxons fought among themselves to establish their individual kingdoms and wealth. As a result they had no unified defence to fend off an outside enemy like the Vikings.

The Vikings would often appear from the sea mist and sail their longships right up onto the beach for a surprise attack. The spread of Christianity in the British

This purse lid from Sutton Hoo, in Suffolk, is the richest of its kind found so far. Items like this were used to display wealth in Anglo-Saxon society.

Isles meant that there were many large and wealthy monasteries which were easy **TARGETS**. The attack on the island **MONASTERY** at Lindisfarne was both unexpected and vicious. It was completely overrun, and many monks were killed and their work destroyed. A contemporary account tells how the people did not know how to respond when Vikings first arrived at Lindisfarne:

"…there came for the first time three ships; and then the reeve rode there and wanted to compel them to go to the king's town, because he did not know what they were; and they killed him. Those were the first ships of the Danish men which sought out the land of the English race."

Source – The Anglo-Saxon Chronicle, written 9th–12th century

[6]

Viking Raids Glossary

bosom	Centre or heart	pagan
contemporary	Occurring at the same time	prow
compel	Force	reeve
ferocity	Fierceness	slayed
navigation	Ability to find the right way	terrain

See also: Saxons and Vikings 4–5; Religion 10–11; Wars and Weapon...

The Glossary explains the meaning of any unusual or difficult words appearing on these two pages

Sub-topic 2 offers complete information about one aspect of the topic

Some suggested words to use in your project

The Case Study is a closer look at a famous person, artefact or building that relates to the topic

Each photo or illustration is described and discussed in its accompanying text

Captions clearly explain what is in the picture

Other pages in the book that relate to what you have read here are listed in this bar

At the bottom of some sections, a reference bar tells you where the quote has come from

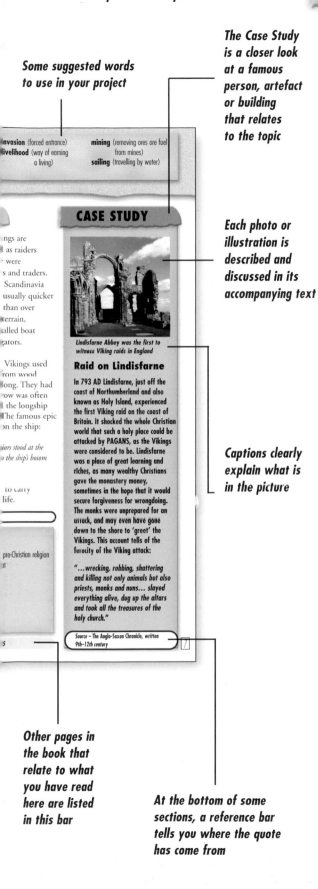

invasion (forced entrance)
livelihood (way of earning a living)

mining (removing ores ore fuel from mines)
sailing (travelling by water)

CASE STUDY

Lindisfarne Abbey was the first to witness Viking raids in England

Raid on Lindisfarne

In 793 AD Lindisfarne, just off the coast of Northumberland and also known as Holy Island, experienced the first Viking raid on the coast of Britain. It shocked the whole Christian world that such a holy place could be attacked by PAGANS, as the Vikings were considered to be. Lindisfarne was a place of great learning and riches, as many wealthy Christians gave the monastery money, sometimes in the hope that it would secure forgiveness for wrongdoing. The monks were unprepared for an attack, and may even have gone down to the shore to 'greet' the Vikings. This account tells of the ferocity of the Viking attack:

"...wrecking, robbing, shattering and killing not only animals but also priests, monks and nuns... slayed everything alive, dug up the altars and took all the treasures of the holy church."

Source – The Anglo-Saxon Chronicle, written 9th–12th century

Keyword Contents

Saxons and Vikings

The departure of the Romans in about 408 AD left Britain undefended. Soon Saxons from Germany began raiding the south of England, and by 600 AD they began to settle, along with other people from Europe, including the Angles from Denmark. For about 200 years the Saxons set up their KINGDOMS. By 789 AD Danish and Norwegian Vikings began to raid the north and east of England, Scotland and Ireland, in search of new land to farm and any wealth they could seize. From this time until the 11th century the Saxons and Vikings ruled Britain.

ALFRED THE GREAT

Saxon warlords fought the Britons and established their own kingdoms. By 700 AD they were in charge of most of England, and by 800 AD had divided it into seven distinct regions, each ruled by its own Saxon king. The area in the south-west was called Wessex.

By this time Danish and Norwegian Vikings had begun raids on the northern and eastern coasts. Individual Viking chiefs led their own raids, but by 865 AD they were fighting as one large army of Danes. As they moved towards unification they became more successful, and defeated some Saxon kings. By 870 AD, the Danes moved south to attack Wessex, and killed King Ethelred at the **BATTLE** of Ashdown in 871 AD. His brother Alfred, aged 21, became king.

In 878 AD Alfred defeated the Danes at the battle of Edington. The historian Asser, Bishop of Sherborne, wrote:

'Alfred attacked the whole pagan army, fighting ferociously in dense order…After fourteen days the pagans were brought to the extreme depths of despair by hunger, cold and fear, and they sought peace.'

Alfred negotiated the peace **TREATY** of Wedmore with the Danish King Guthrum. By 886 AD England was divided into the Viking-ruled Danelaw in the north, while Alfred increased the area he ruled to include West Mercia, Sussex and Kent.

Legend says that Alfred, preoccupied with the defence of his kingdom, burned some cakes, which he had been asked to look after.

Source – The Life of King Alfred, by Asser, Bishop of Sherborne, 893 AD

Words to use in your project

age (period of time)
blockade (barricade)
council (gathering)

dominion (a governed territory or country)
hostility (a feeling of enmity)

idolatry (worshipping an idol or idols)
sovereign (supreme monarch)

KING CANUTE

Alfred died in 899 AD. His successor Ethelred The Unready was a weak king, who had been paying bribes to stop Danish attacks. These bribes were raised through taxes and known as the Danegeld. In 1002 AD Ethelred ordered the massacre of the Danes in England, including the sister of the Viking King Sweyn Forkbeard. Sweyn overthrew Ethelred in 1013 AD, but died shortly after. Sweyn's son, Canute, took the throne in 1016 AD. He successfully ruled an **EMPIRE** that covered England, Denmark, Norway and Sweden. Canute established an era of **PEACE** and prosperity, and encouraged trade, religion, justice and artistic work. According to legend, he sat on the beach and waited for the tide to come in. This was to show that there were things not even he could control.

King Canute waits for the tide to come in.

Source – The Anglo-Saxon Chronicle, written 9th–12th century

Saxons and Vikings Glossary

empire	Many countries under one ruler	**pagan**	Follower of a pre-Christian religion
massacre	The deliberate killing of lots of people	**plunder**	Rob or loot
		prosperity	Wealth
Mercia	Saxon kingdom, now the Midlands area of England	**treaty**	A peace agreement
		unification	Become one
negotiate	Discuss to try to reach an agreement	**warlord**	Regional leader of a military force

See also: Viking Raids 6–7; Economy 14–15; Wars and Weapons 20–21; Language 22–23

CASE STUDY

Treaty of Wedmore

After the battle of Edington, Alfred and King Guthrum drew up the Treaty of Wedmore that divided the country and created the DANELAW. Alfred insisted that Guthrum and his chief men should become Christian. At the time of the Viking invasions Britain had many Christian missionaries and monasteries. For a long time, the Viking invaders had been targeting the poorly-defended monasteries, such as Lindisfarne off the north east coast, and plundering their riches. Although the Vikings had their own religion and many gods, many were happy to accept Christianity. This is an account of Guthrum's baptism:

"Then the army gave him hostages with many oaths, that they would go out of his kingdom. They told him also, that their king would receive baptism… King Guthrum, attended by some thirty of the worthiest men that were in the army, came to him… and there the king became his sponsor in baptism."

Source – The Anglo-Saxon Chronicle, written 9th–12th century

Viking Raids

Vikings originated in the Scandinavian countries of Denmark, Sweden and Norway. Their countries were hilly, covered in forests and not always good for farming. As their population grew there was not enough land for everyone, so they were forced to carry out raids on neighbouring countries in northern Europe. Their boat-building and navigation skills meant that they soon started raiding the British Isles. They made swift ATTACKS on coastal areas, targeting monasteries, stealing treasures and capturing slaves.

CAUSES OF RAIDS

After the Romans departed, it was not long before the Saxons started invading and settling. The native Britons had their own **TERRITORIES** which they fought hard to protect. As well as fighting the Britons, the Saxons fought among themselves to establish their individual kingdoms and wealth. As a result they had no unified defence to fend off an outside enemy like the Vikings.

The Vikings would often appear from the sea mist and sail their longships right up onto the beach for a surprise attack. The spread of Christianity in the British Isles meant that there were many large and wealthy monasteries which were easy **TARGETS**. The attack on the island **MONASTERY** at Lindisfarne was both unexpected and vicious. It was completely overrun, and many monks were killed and their work destroyed. A contemporary account tells how the people did not know how to respond when Vikings first arrived at Lindisfarne:

"…there came for the first time three ships; and then the reeve rode there and wanted to compel them to go to the king's town, because he did not know what they were; and they killed him. Those were the first ships of the Danish men which sought out the land of the English race."

This purse lid from Sutton Hoo, in Suffolk, is the richest of its kind found so far. Items like this were used to display wealth in Anglo-Saxon society.

 Source – The Anglo-Saxon Chronicle, written 9th–12th century

SHIPS

Vikings had the advantage of fast ships, which they used to raid neighbouring countries.

Although the Vikings are often remembered as raiders and invaders, they were also great explorers and traders. The geography of Scandinavia meant that it was usually quicker to travel by water than over the mountainous terrain, so Vikings were skilled boat builders and navigators.

The **LONGSHIPS** Vikings used for raiding were made from wood and could be up to 30 metres long. They had sails, but could also be rowed. The prow was often decorated with a frightening carving, and the longship was protected with shields down each side. The famous epic poem *Beowulf* describes the **WEAPONS** kept on the ship:

"They readied the ship on the waves under the cliffs and the warriors stood at the prow as the water wound against the sand. The warriors bore into the ship's bosom bright weapons, fitted armour."

An important Viking might be buried with his ship to carry him and the possessions he would need in the next life.

Source – Beowulf, written down about 1000 AD

Viking Raids Glossary

bosom	Centre or heart	**pagan**	Follower of a pre-Christian religion
contemporary	Occurring at the same time	**prow**	Front of a boat
compel	Force	**reeve**	Town official
ferocity	Fierceness	**slayed**	Killed
navigation	Ability to find the right way	**terrain**	Ground

CASE STUDY

Lindisfarne Abbey was the first to witness Viking raids in England

Raid on Lindisfarne

In 793 AD Lindisfarne, just off the coast of Northumberland and also known as Holy Island, experienced the first Viking raid on the coast of Britain. It shocked the whole Christian world that such a holy place could be attacked by PAGANS, as the Vikings were considered to be. Lindisfarne was a place of great learning and riches, as many wealthy Christians gave the monastery money, sometimes in the hope that it would secure forgiveness for wrongdoing. The monks were unprepared for an attack, and may even have gone down to the shore to 'greet' the Vikings. This account tells of the ferocity of the Viking attack:

"...wrecking, robbing, shattering and killing not only animals but also priests, monks and nuns... slayed everything alive, dug up the altars and took all the treasures of the holy church."

Source – The Anglo-Saxon Chronicle, written 9th–12th century

Administration

Each Saxon region had its own rules. The Danelaw was governed by Viking rules. Early laws tended to be a set of punishments for crimes, rather than rules for living a good life. The laws of the Kentish king Ethelbert (601–604 AD) were the first that were clearly not Roman. Later that century, the laws of Ine, king of southern England, introduced new ideas, including that of a free PEASANT who was master of his own house, and a social order that included an ARISTOCRACY.

KINGSHIP

During the reign of King Alfred the power of a king evolved. Up to this point, separate kingdoms had been governed in different ways. Alfred realised that strength came from unity. After his success at Edington, his influence extended further than his original territory of Wessex and he became recognised as the first king of England.

Alfred saw the importance of allowing people to continue with their farming and trade while making sure that they were well defended. He built a system of burhs (defensive market towns) across southern England, and people received plots of land in return for their willingness to fight. His army consisted of his thegns (royal followers) as well as the fyrd (professional warriors).In 890 AD, Alfred wrote:

"No man, as you know can…conduct or administer government, unless he has fit tools…I mean that which is necessary to the exercise of natural powers; thus a king's raw material and instruments of rule are a well-peopled land, and he must have men of prayer, men of war, and men of work."

Alfred's son, Edward, continued to unify the rule by forming strong **ALLIANCES** with other Saxon leaders, and by gaining the respect of the Vikings. He was able to develop administrative practices for what was becoming the unified country of England.

These 9th-century rings were probably symbols of royal office.

Source – The Anglo-Saxon Chronicle, written 9th–12th century

Words to use in your project

concede (yield, grant)
dominate (rule)
enactment (enacted, as a law)

execute (To carry out orders)
mandate (authoritative order or command)

reorganize (restructure)
violator (a person failing to comply with law)

VIKING TINGS

Early Viking culture allowed members of a 'tribe' to seek vengeance if one of their own people was killed or injured. The Viking Ting, also known as a Thing or Althing, was introduced as a way to make local rules, and also to judge people accused of doing wrong. Ting members were free men of the community. Meetings were held regularly in a public area, and could last all day.

Larger areas might have Tings comprised of representatives from local Tings. The Ting developed further into a way of solving **DISPUTES**, making laws, electing chiefs and taking **POLITICAL DECISIONS**. Laws were not written, but memorised and recited by the speaker (judge).

The power of Tings are shown in this passage:

"Then King Canute proceeded; and, to be short in our tale, did not stop until he came to Trondheim, and landed at Nidaros. In Trondheim he called together a Thing for the eight districts, at which King Canute was chosen king of all Norway."

Thingvellir in Iceland has been the country's main meeting place since Viking times.

Source – The Anglo-Saxon Chronicle, written 9th–12th century

Administration Glossary

administrative	Relating to organisation	**grievance**	Problem
alliance	Agreement to help each other	**proclaim**	Announce
		recited	Spoken
aristocracy	Ruling class	**tribe**	A set of people
Danelaw	Area of northern England ruled by the Vikings	**vengeance**	Revenge
		Wessex	Area of southern England
disputes	Disagreements		

See also: Saxons and Vikings 4–5; Society 12–13; Family and Marriage 18–19; Law and Justice 28–29

CASE STUDY

Regular Tings met at Tynwald Hill on the Isle of Man (a Viking colony).

Manx Tynwald

Many modern assemblies and **PARLIAMENTS** are directly descended from the Viking Tings, including Norway's Storting, Greenland's Landsting and the Isle of Man's Tynwald. The High Court of Tynwald is the oldest continuous parliament in the world. It has two branches, the Legislative Council and the House of Keys. Every year on about July 5 members of both houses meet at the traditional open-air site of St John's at Tynwald Hill. All Isle of Man residents can attend. At the ceremony it is still the duty of the Deemsters (chief judges) to formally proclaim the Acts of Tynwald by reading the title of each, with a short statement about it in both Manx and English so that they may become law. On this day all people of the Isle of Man can state their grievances.

Source – http://www.isleofman.com

Religion

The Christian FAITH had been introduced to Britain in Roman times, and an influential monastery was founded in 563 AD by Columba on Iona, an island off Scotland's west coast. When the Saxons arrived in Britain they WORSHIPPED many different gods and GODDESSES, each to do with a different aspect of life. In 597 AD Pope Gregory sent the monk Augustine to Britain, on a mission to convert the Saxon leaders to Christianity. The Vikings also had their own gods and goddesses, some very similar to the Saxon ones.

MONASTIC REFORMS

When Augustine arrived with his Benedictine monks, King Ethelbert let them stay in Kent. Ethelbert's wife, Bertha, was already a Christian, and soon he was converted and **BAPTISED**. This inspired many of his followers, so Christianity spread in southern England. Within ten years, Christianity was the official religion of Kent, Sussex and London. Monasteries were built in Canterbury, Rochester and London, and Canterbury soon became the southern centre for Christianity.

At about the same time, the work of Columba and his monks spread down from Scotland into northern England. In 635 AD the monk, Aidan, came down from Iona and set up a base at Lindisfarne island, on the coast of Northumberland. Eventually, Christianity moved further south to Jarrow, Ripon, Whitby and Durham and more monasteries were built.

The functions of church and state became closely interwoven during this period. The monasteries were places of learning and the monks also cared for local people. They soon became wealthy from gifts given to them. Here Bede describes the early days of Christianity:

"...those among them who had received priest's orders administered to the believers the grace of baptism. Churches were built in several places; the people joyfully flocked together to hear the Word; possessions and lands were given of the King's bounty to build monasteries;

Lindisfarne Castle on Lindisfarne island.

Source – The Anglo-Saxon Chronicle, written 9th–12th century

VIKING GODS

The Vikings, like the Saxons, had many different gods and goddesses. They were split into two families called Vanir and Asar, and lived in a place called Asgard that was joined to Midgard (earth) by the rainbow bridge Bifrost. For Viking warriors a heroic death meant they would go to Valhalla, the palace of bliss. Dying in bed meant you ended up in Hiflheim, the depths of the earth.

Odin was the most important Viking god. Two ravens, Hugin (thought) and Munin (Memory), sat on his shoulders and brought him knowledge from their journeys. Another important god was Thor, the god of thunder. He was a huge, strong god with a bright red beard and he had a magic hammer, Mjollnir. He was also the god of law and order, the champion of the people. Thor was always true, so oaths were often sworn in Thor's name.

A Viking carving of the god Thor.

Religion Glossary

administered	Given	**bounty**	Generosity
archaeologist	A person who examines objects from the past to see how people used to live	**convert**	A change in religious belief
		interwoven	Closely connected
		Iona	An island off the coast of Scotland
Benedictine	A group of monks who followed the teachings of Saint Benedict	**oath**	A promise something is true
		possessions	Things owned by somebody

See also: Administration 8–9; Food and Drink 16–17; Towns 24–25; Architecture and Art 26–27

CASE STUDY

Burials

Vikings believed that a person's **SPIRIT** sailed to the next life. There and on the journey, they would need certain possessions, which were buried with them. A Viking might be buried with a ship, or sent to sea in a burning longship. Some graves were just marked with stones in the shape of a longship. Arab chronicler Ibn Fadlan described a Viking burial:

If the deceased is a poor man they make a little boat, which they lay him in and burn. If he is rich... I saw that they had drawn the ship onto the shore, and that they had erected four posts of birch wood... Then they pulled the ship up until it was on this wooden construction. and set the ship on fire, so that the dead man and the ship are shortly burned to ashes.

Differences in types of **BURIALS** has made it easier for archaeologists to trace the spread of Christianity.

Dead Viking warriors were often burned on their longships at sea.

Source – Ibn Fadlan, written after a voyage in 921 AD.

Society

Saxon England was based on a rural lifestyle and there were three broad classes of people: rulers, free people and slaves. Within each of these groups there were further divisions, and a person had responsibilities according to his STATUS, such as providing food for others or being prepared to fight in times of unrest. Viking society was also divided into three similar areas.

During Saxon times, market towns or burhs started to grow, and trade became increasingly important, though farming remained the main part of the economy.

RICH AND POOR

The most important Saxons were the kings, and their princes (æðelings) who could claim a family link with the king. The idea that a king's son would **INHERIT** his position became more established with King Alfred, but the council of elders, or witan, still had the right to choose.

A ruling noble called an eolderman kept law and justice in his area. He would summon the fyrd (professional warriors) and lead them in battle. His title was not automatically passed down to members of his family.

There were many types of thegn (also known as thane) and higher thegns could become eoldermen. Thegns might have their own land, or simply look after some of the king's land. They were the main professional warriors of the fyrd. The king had thegns who were directly responsible to him, and so did eoldermen. A higher thegn could have his own thegns.

Ceorls were freemen, farmers and people who owned small areas of land. Their work contributed most to the local economy. **SLAVES** or bondsmen had to work for their master, but they could own property and earn money in their own time. They tended to be looked after, as this extract tells:

"If a lord has his theow [slave] to work on a festival day let him pay lahsit within the Danish law, and wite among the English."

This 10th century Viking arm-ring would have been worn by a rich person as a way to display their wealth and status.

Source – The Laws of Alfred, Guthrum, and Edward the Elder, c. 10th Century

Words to use in your project

adversary (rival)
commerce (buying and selling)
hierarchy (according to status)

occupation (a vocation)
pastoral (associated with country life)

regulated (controlled)
traders (persons engaged in commerce)

FARMERS AND TRADERS

Vikings and Saxons farmed the land and lived off the food they grew and animals they reared. Farms were run by a **FAMILY**, sometimes with the help of peasants or slaves. The work was very hard.

Most Vikings were full-time farmers and only part-time warriors.

> *"Ploughman: Oh my lord, I work very hard: I go out at dawn, driving the cattle to the field, and I yoke them to the plough. Nor is the weather so bad in winter that I dare to stay at home, for fear of my lord: but ...I must plough one whole field a day, or more... it is a great labour for I am not free."*

Trade was an important part of both Saxon and Viking society. Although Vikings had a reputation for being warriors they also had well-established trade routes with eastern European and Middle Eastern countries. Market towns (burhs) developed during Alfred's reign as places where farmers, craftsmen and merchants could trade safely. There were coins in Saxon and Viking times, but the barter system was often used at markets. The king raised taxes by taking some of the money made by traders.

Source – Ælfric's Colloquy, written about 1000 AD

Society Glossary

barter	Trade by exchanging goods	**livestock**	Farm animals
compensation		**status**	Position
	Something given to make up for a loss	**lahsit**	A fine
		tilled	Ploughed
lahsit	A fine	**wite**	A fine
lay	Not to do with religion	**yoke**	Harness
levies	Fighting force		

See also: Viking Raids 6–7; Economy 14–15; Language 22–23; Sports and Pastimes 30–31

CASE STUDY

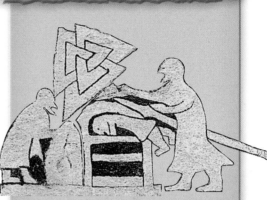

Public killings were also used for vengeance, as seen on this picture stone from Lärbro parish of Gotland.

Wergild and revenge

Both Saxon and Viking society had a system known as wergild, or blood money. It was a way to make sure that people were not killed as **REVENGE** for some wrong that had been done. If a Viking's slave was killed, he could claim a certain amount of money or livestock from the murderer. Wergild also provided compensation for the families of Saxon thegns and ceorls killed in battle. An agreed price would be paid out for the death of a man. The amount was set according to his wealth and social status.

Revenge was a common part of Viking life, with family honour being very important. A disgrace to a man or his family was intolerable and revenge was seen as the only way to restore **HONOUR**. This view of revenge is given in the Viking saying:

"A slave takes revenge at once, a fool never takes revenge."

Source – Viking proverb

Economy

Most of the trade and wealth in early Saxon times was created through agriculture. Farmers sold their SURPLUS stock at market and towns developed as major trading centres. The Viking town of Jorvik (now York) was one of the biggest trading towns of the period. Laws regulated buying and selling in the towns, and were a way of raising taxes. Although the barter system was widely used, trade also helped to establish the use of coins. By 928 AD England had a single CURRENCY based on the penny.

TRADING

If a farmer had more grain, livestock or other produce than he needed, he could sell or exchange them for other **COMMODITIES** at the market. The goods could include wares produced by craftsmen, such as metalwork, pottery or cloth. Some of these things were made locally, but gradually more items from Europe were brought in to be traded, including furs, glassware and swords.

Getting goods to and from the market towns could be dangerous and difficult. Roads were not very good, and ambush by robbers was common. Transporting goods by water was preferred, so successful markets were usually near rivers.

Traders preferred to take their goods to market by boat as it was cheaper and quicker than the roads, although not always safer.

The building of **BURHS** or burghs (market towns with strong defensive walls) made trade safer, and some also became the site of **MINTS**. Buying was carefully regulated, as can be seen in this 10th century law:

"And that no man buy out of port, but have the port-reeve's witness, or that of other unlying men whom one may believe. And if any one buy out of port then let him incur the king's oferhyrnes..."

Overseas trade was common for the Vikings who had many established routes and contacts. The prosperity of Jorvik (York) and its importance as a trading centre grew. In 1000 AD an unknown writer described it as:

"...filled with the treasure of merchants, principally Danes."

Source – The Laws of King Edward the Elder, 901-924 AD

Words to use in your project

coinage (different coins)
craft (make with skill)

export (send goods to other countries)
import (bring in goods from other countries)

ownership (having possession of)

COINS

COINS had been used by Romans, but for 200 years after their departure they were hardly used. The first Saxon coins, thrysmas, were made of gold but copied

The Saxon kings needed more and more mints to pay for war against Vikings.

from Roman bronze coins. The first real Saxon coins, sceattas, were made of silver from about 600 AD. Their value and appearance varied throughout the country. The penny was

introduced to southern England in about 764 AD and over time became the dominant currency. Pennies showed an image of the Saxon king.

Viking rulers also produced large numbers of coins for their trade. The Vikings in Britain soon followed the Saxons and minted coins that showed their own rulers. Jorvik became an important mint. King Athelstan passed this law in 928 AD stating that there was to be only a single currency in England:

"…that there be one money over all the king's dominion, and that no man mint except within port. And if the moneyer be guilty, let the hand be struck off that wrought the offence, and, be set up on the money-smithy…"

Source – The Laws of King Athelstan, 924–939 AD

Economy Glossary

currency	A system of money	**oferhymes**	Punishment
dominant	Main	**offence**	The act of breaking a law
dominion	Area controlled by a king	**overseas**	Across the sea
exchange	Give something in return for something else	**regulated**	Controlled
		surplus	Amount above what is needed
mint	A place where coins are made		

See also: Administration 8–9; Religion 10–11; Food and Drink 16–17; Law and Justice 28–29

CASE STUDY

A man dressed in the clothing of a typical Saxon slave.

Slavery

Like the Romans before them, Saxons and Vikings had slaves. A Viking slave was called a thrall (male) or Ambatt (female). Viking slaves were often people captured during raids. The trade in slaves with Eastern European and Middle Eastern countries brought a lot of money to the economy.

Saxon slaves were called deow, and they had a number of rights, including that of buying their freedom. A master had responsibilities towards slaves, and would sometimes free them under the terms of his will. As slaves had food and shelter, peasants who hit hard times would sometimes sell themselves into **SLAVERY**. The rights of slaves were detailed in the laws of King Alfred:

"All slaves ought to have Christmas supplies and Easter supplies, an acre for the plough and a 'handful of the harvest', in addition to their necessary rights."

Source – The Laws of King Alfred, 871–899 AD

Food and Drink

The STAPLE diet for people at this time included meat, fish, vegetables, bread, fruits and GRAINS. Most food was cooked in a large pot hung over an open fire, usually as a stew that could be eaten with bread. Food was also cooked in the embers of the fire, wrapped in clay or leaves to protect it. Saxons and Vikings usually ate from a wooden bowl or plate using only a knife, spoon or eating stick – and of course their fingers! Apart from water they drank beer and MEAD, a type of beer made from honey and barley. Wooden or pottery cups were used for drinking.

THE SAXON DIET

Saxon food came from three main sources. Most families farmed the food they needed, by growing **CROPS** and rearing animals. They also hunted animals and fish, and gathered wild fruits and vegetables. If they could afford to, they would trade at the market for other items they needed.

Everything they ate was made by themselves, so they ground the wheat they had grown into flour and made it into bread. They were dependent on **SEASONAL** food that was available according to the time of year, as many kinds of food could not be **PRESERVED**. As well as grains such as wheat, barley and oats, they also grew some vegetables including carrots, cabbages, onions and garlic. They flavoured foods with herbs. Sugar was not available so honey was used to sweeten foods and most Saxons kept their own bees.

Both Vikings and Saxons were expert fishermen, and used nets, spears and hooked lines. A lot of their fishing was in rivers and streams, but they also fished out at sea. They ate herring, salmon, eel, pike and perch, as well as shellfish. Some fish are mentioned in Ælfric's Colloquy:

"Master: Which fish do you catch?
Fisherman: Eels and pike, minnows and turbot,
trout and lampreys and whatever swims in the water."

Eels were among the fish eaten by the Saxons.

Source – Ælfric's Colloquy, written about 1000 AD

THE VIKING DIET

Meat, milk, eggs, wool and leather came from the cows, goats, pigs, sheep, chicken ducks and geese that were kept. They also hunted birds, deer, hares and boar.

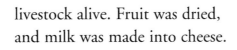

Viking people hunted deer for meat.

Meat was usually stewed. Only wealthy people could afford to roast meat on a metal spit over a fire, as it used far more fuel.

It was important to preserve meat and fish by smoking, drying or salting, so there was enough food to last through the winter. As the winter progressed, more animals were killed, as this meant fresh food for the family as well as less feed to keep the livestock alive. Fruit was dried, and milk was made into cheese.

Although both Vikings and Saxons made lots of beer, heavy drinking was not encouraged, as seen in this traditional advice:

"Drink your mead, but in moderation,
Talk sense or be silent:
No man is called discourteous
Who goes to bed at an early hour."

> Source – The poetic Edda, a book of Viking poems and lore, c. 1250

Food and Drink Glossary

aristocracy	Ruling class of people	**preserved**	Saved
ember	A glowing piece of coal or wood	**prestige**	Status
		seasonal	According to the time of year
herb	Plant used to flavour food or treat ailments	**staple**	Main
		theowman	Slave
hide	Area of land	**wite**	A fine
moderation	A normal amount		

CASE STUDY

Feasting

Feasts were held to celebrate holy days and special events including weddings. For the rich they were also used as a show of prestige, and were surrounded with etiquette and rituals, such as handwashing and who sat next to one another. Often guests were not allowed to leave the table until all the food was eaten. Feasting was regulated by laws:

"If a freeman break a lawful feast, let him pay wite or lahslit. If a theowman do so, let him suffer in his hide or hide-gild."

A 11th century carving showing a typical Viking banquet.

It was not unusual for a feast to last several days. Everyone, not just the aristocracy, enjoyed feasts. Often, large tables heaving with food and drink. Slaves were allowed to join in some of feasting.

Preparing a large feast could be complicated as the ovens in Saxon manors were communal, and food storage was difficult.

> Source – The Laws of Alfred, Guthrum, and Edward the Elder, c. 10th Century

See also: Society 12–13; Economy 14–15; Architecture and Art 26–27; Sports and Pastimes 30–31

Family and Marriage

Vikings lived in large family groups or extended families, with several GENERATIONS together in the same house. Servants or slaves usually lived in the house too. Saxons also lived in extended families, and formed small SETTLEMENTS by building their homes close together. During the day men and women, with their children, spent most of their time on basic needs like growing and cooking food, making yarn and clothes, and various crafts. From the age of about five, children worked with adults to learn life skills.

MARRIAGE

Men and women were often married at between 12 and 15 years old. Saxon and Viking marriages were more about forming **ALLIANCES** and regulating relationships than falling in love. Often families would agree the marriage, and the bride and groom had to make it a success as much for the future of their families as for their own happiness. Stories from the time suggest that the girl was consulted before betrothal but that if she said no the marriage might still happen. For rich and powerful families the terms of morgengifu (literally, 'morning gift'), money, **DOWRY** and other riches the two parties would bring to the marriage needed to be settled before the wedding.

Saxon women could own and manage land and **PROPERTY** and retained many rights even after marriage. After marriage, money and property belonged jointly to husband and wife. **OATHS** and marriage vows were taken seriously as this passage from the law of King Alfred shows:

Marriage in Viking society was a family affair. The extended family looked after women and children should a husband be killed.

"…it is most needful that every man warily keep his oath and his wed… if he pledge himself to that which it is lawful to fulfil, and in that belie himself… let him there suffer whatever the bishop may prescribe to him…"

Source – The Laws of King Alfred, 871–899 AD

Words to use in your project	arranged (planned)	sanctuary (place of safety)	spouse (marriage partner)
	customs (traditions)	settlement (group of homes; village)	
	childbirth (producing a baby)		

DAILY LIFE

Viking longhouses were rectangular with just one room, similar to this cottage in the Shetland Islands today.

Most Vikings were farmers and lived in small countryside settlements. They attached great importance to their home, as this quote shows:

*"A small hut of one's own is better,
A man is his master at home:
A couple of goats and a corded roof
Still are better than begging."*

Vikings built longhouses, usually just one long room where the whole family ate and slept. The size depended on how rich the family was. A longhouse was made of wood with a turf roof. It was dark and smoky inside as there were no windows and no chimney, just a hole in the roof. A lot of work was done outside. There might also be places for animals to shelter and a small smithy. A wall or fence would keep animals in and enemies out. Many Viking longhouses survive on the Shetland Isles, where they were built on low stone foundations.

Source – Hávamál, a book of poems and advice, c. 950 AD

Family and Marriage Glossary

alliance	Joining by marriage, treaty or agreement	**morgengifu**	Money or property settled on a wife by her new husband
betrothal	Engagement to be married	**smithy**	A place for working with metal
dowry	Money or property paid by a woman's family to her new husband	**turf**	A slab of grass and earth
foundations	The base of a house	**yarn**	Spun fibre for making cloth

See also: Religion 10–11; Language 22–23; Towns 24–25; Law and Justice 28–29

CASE STUDY

A woman's role

The role of women in these times was to run the house, which was a substantial and important job. Depending on her social class a woman might have slaves or servants to help her to prepare food, make yarn to weave fabric and look after the farm or property in her husband's absence. She would also take charge of the health of her family, including preparing herbal medicines.

Women were at great risk during childbirth as pregnancy was not fully understood. This is an example of advice given to pregnant women:

"...ought to be fully warned against eating anything too salt or too sweet, and against drinking strong alcohol: also against pork and fatty foods; also against drinking to the point of drunkenness, also against travelling; also against too much riding on horseback lest the child is born before the right time."

Viking women adorned their long hair with combs.

Source – Bald's Leechbook, c. 900 AD

Wars and Weapons

The reputation of a ruler, and the territory he held, depended on his ability to win battles. Each ruler had his own band of warriors, who might be fighting men from the area or professional MERCENARIES. The ruler relied on his thegns to help him lead them into battle. A fighting force of able men, known as the fyrd, could be called to fight when needed. After King Alfred's victory in 878 AD, military organisation became more unified. Spears, swords and axes were common weapons, with shields used for protection.

MILITARY ORGANISATION

Each Saxon ruler had a **FYRD**, or fighting force, with which to defend his own land, or attack another area. These fyrds were often fairly small. The warriors were loyal to their chief, and if he was killed it was their duty to seek **REVENGE**. Until the Vikings invaded, the main enemies of Saxon rulers were other Saxon rulers. Viking chiefs had similar bands of **WARRIORS**, called hirð. who were loyal to their lords.

The fyrd became a well organised way to raise a fighting force quickly. The number of freemen (usually thegns or ceorls) called to serve depended on the size of the area, and there was a rota system that reduced the burden on estates. This ensured that there were enough people left in the countryside to keep producing the food that was essential for feeding the people as well as the fyrd. From the early 9th century, the fyrd was regulated, as this account tells us:

"The king divided his army into two, so that always half of its men were at home, half on service, apart from the men who guarded the boroughs."

In peacetime the fyrd served one month in three so there was always a force on hand. They also carried out police work and built town defences. There was a shift to a more permanent army by the 11th century.

The section of the Bayeux Tapestry (1050–1097) illustrates the 'shield-wall' formed by the Anglo-Saxon military during the Battle of Hastings.

| Source – The Anglo-Saxon Chronicle, written 9th–12th century

Words to use in your project

allegiance (loyalty)
bodyguard (armed troops that protect an important person)

chivalry (valour)
conquer (overcome and gain control)

courage (bravery)
infantry (soldiers marching or fighting on foot)

WEAPONS AND ARMOUR

Heavy axes made better weapons for attack than defence.

All men were expected to be armed, and the most common and effective weapon was the spear. It was used by all classes of men and had a metal tip on a wooden shaft. The size and shape depended on whether it was to be used for throwing or thrusting.

The most prized weapon was the sword, often handed down from father to son. Its importance is related in *Beowulf*:

"Beowulf… then spoke some brave words before he got in bed, I don't claim myself any lower in strength or brave deeds than Grendel. Therefore, I will not kill him with a sword, though I easily might."

Other weapons included heavy axes and rounded stones and other **MISSILES** that could be thrown. The shafts of spears, swords and axes were often intricately carved or inlaid to show the owner's wealth and status.

HELMETS were made from thick leather. No other armour was worn, but a strong shield provided some protection. Soldiers learned to overlap their shields to produce a defensive wall which was hard to breach.

Source – Beowulf, written down about 1000 AD

Wars and Weapons Glossary

breach	Make a gap	**shaft**	Handle
ceorl	An ordinary freeman	**slain**	Killed
mercenary	Paid soldier	**thegn**	Fighting man
Normandy	Area of northern France	**thither**	Here
professional	To earn a living from an activity	**warrior**	Person experienced in conflict
rota	System of regular change	**Witan**	Saxon ruling council

See also: Viking Raids 6–7; Administration 8–9; Society 12–13; Law and Justice 28–29

CASE STUDY

This wall-hanging made by an unknown artist depicts the Battle of Hastings.

The Battle of Hastings

Edward the Confessor died in 1065, and the Witan named Harold, Edward's brother-in-law, king. Harald Hardrada of Norway, sometimes called Harald Fairhair, saw his chance and landed an army in Yorkshire in September 1066. Harold defeated the Vikings at Stamford Bridge, as this account tells:

"Thither came Harold, king of the English, unawares against them beyond the bridge; and they closed together there, and continued long in the day fighting very severely. There was slain Harald the Fair-hair'd, King of Norway."

Within days, Harold had a new enemy to face. Duke William of Normandy landed his men in southern England, claiming that Edward the Confessor had promised him the English throne. Harold returned south with his exhausted army and met William at the Battle of Hastings on October 14. The Normans, with their superior archers and cavalry, won. Harold was killed.

Source – The Anglo-Saxon Chronicle, written 9th–12th century

Language

No single language was spoken during the 600 years of Saxon and Viking Britain. OLD ENGLISH is the general name for the various DIALECTS spoken by the Saxons, which evolved from the Germanic languages they brought with them. Some of the Celtic language spoken by native Britons was incorporated into Old English. The Vikings spoke many dialects of OLD NORSE, and when they invaded, this influenced the language spoken in Britain and changed still further.

OLD ENGLISH

Old English and Old Norse had many words in common. For example, the Old English word for a child was 'bearn' while the most common Old Norse word for child was 'barn'. The same word, 'bairn', is still used in Scotland and northern England. If there was no Old English equivalent for a word in Old Norse, the language of the invader was simply added.

Many Saxon first names, including Edmund, Agnes and Edith are still in use today. A surname might relate to where a person came from. For example, Matilda who lived in Chichester would be known as Matilda of Chichester, or just Matilda Chichester. Job-related surnames including Baker, Weaver, Fisher, Fowler and Hunter have also survived. A Viking surname showed the name of his mother or father, so Harald, son of Eric, would be Harald Eriksson.

Old English can be hard to understand, but if you read a translation, many words become clearer.

Old English alphabets were significantly different from those of modern English.

[Teacher]: Hwæt hæfst ͜u weorkes?
[Pupil]: Ic eom geanwyrde monuc, ond sincge ælce dæg seofon tida mid gebro͜rum, ac ͜eahhwæ͜ere ic wolde hetwenan leorniun sprecan on leden gereorde.

[Teacher]: What is your work?
[Pupil]: I am a professed monk, and sing every day seven times with the brethren, and I am busy, but nevertheless, between-times I learn to speak the Latin language.

Source – Ælfric's Colloquy, written about 1000 AD

Words to use in your project

ancestor (person from whom another is descended)
dialect (a regional form of language)

mother tongue (native language)
mythology (stories and legends of a culture)

nostalgia (affection for the past)
oral tradition (remembering and telling stories)

ANGLO SAXON POETRY

Old English **POETRY** often told heroic tales of Saxon or Viking history, or Christian stories of morals and beliefs.

The epic *Beowulf* is one of the oldest poems written in England. Many poems were never written down, but were recited by the poet or scop. A scop would often memorise hundreds of lines of poetry about battles and other adventures. This provided entertainment and also ensured that history was passed on. Most of the literature that does survive was written down by monks.

Many Old English poems, including *Beowulf*, *Widsith*, *Deor* and *The Wanderer*, tell of the past and compare it to the difficulties of present life. Sometimes there is a Christian

Widsith is one of the earliest Old English poems, written about the 7th century.

message that offers some consolation. *The Seafarer* presents a particularly bleak picture of a world that has lost its splendour, and in which the 'good old days' are no more. The narrator moans:

"Now there are no captains or kings, or gold-givers as there once were, when they did most glorious deeds .. .joys have departed; the weak remain to rule this world..."

Source – The Seafarer, an Anglo-Saxon poem, c.970 AD

Language Glossary

bleak	Depressing	**Latin**	The language that used to be used for religious ceremonies
brethren	Monks		
dialect	Local language or speech	**literature**	Written works that are highly regarded
fowler	Hunter of birds		
Germanic	Relating to Germany	**oral**	Spoken
hieroglyphics		**professed**	Person in a religious order
	Picture representing a word or sound	**recite**	Speak aloud

CASE STUDY

Runes are a key to understanding the lives and beliefs of the ancient people.

Runes

Most Vikings and Saxons could not read or write, so the **ORAL TRADITION** of reciting remembered stories was the only way to pass on information. Symbols called **RUNES** were used, but these were more like hieroglyphics than modern letters, as each had a separate meaning.

Runes had religious significance and were often carved on grave markers. Memorial stones, telling of heroic deeds, were also carved with runes and placed in a public place.

The Vikings and Saxons considered runes to be magical. They were used to tell the future and cast spells. The poem Havamal shows how a man used runes to raise a ghost:

*"A twelfth [spell] I know:
when I see aloft upon a tree
A corpse swinging from a rope,
Then I cut and paint runes
So that the man walks
And speaks with me."*

Source – Hávamál, a book of poems and advice, c. 950 AD

See also: Food and Drink 16–17; Wars and Weapons 20–21; Architecture and Art 26–27

Towns

The Saxons added to Roman towns and also built new ones for defensive purposes. When King Alfred planned to build a string of FORTIFIED towns or burhs, he realised that this could protect his kingdom from invading armies, as well as providing safe places to live and trade. Towns contained market places, workshops, mints, ADMINISTRATIVE centres and garrisons for soldiers. Vikings tended to live in the countryside, but they soon developed Jorvik (York) into a major town for trade and commerce.

LIFE IN TOWNS

Saxon towns developed because of the need for local markets and fairs, and centres for worship and justice. Roman towns were still used, but new towns also developed as Saxon leaders travelled throughout their areas to collect taxes and sort out disputes. The name 'tun' was used for these new towns or places.

Towns were also places of safety as many were surrounded by a **DEFENSIVE** wall or fence. People from outlying areas were allowed in during times of danger. Alfred's plan for 33 burhs or defended areas, mostly along the border with the Danelaw, meant that most people were within 20 miles of a safe **HAVEN**. The chronicler Asser describes the work of building and rebuilding work during Alfred's reign:

"...the towns and cities he restored, and others which he built where none had been before."

Warfare meant that towns were sometimes destroyed and had to be rebuilt, as with this description of London in 886 AD:

"Alfred... after the burning of the cities and the slaying of the people, honourably rebuilt the city of London, and made it again habitable."

The Vikings also developed towns as centres of trade and commerce. Some towns, such as Jorvik, had goods coming in from Scandinavia and other parts of Europe, and from Russia, Central Asia and the Middle East.

Viking settlements were often small groups of homes surrounded by a wooden fence.

Source – The Life of King Alfred, by Asser, Bishop of Sherborne, 893 AD

LONDON AND YORK

This reconstruction of Jorvik shows its streets filled with merchants and traders, just as it would have been in Viking times.

Jorvik (York) grew to be the major town in the Danelaw and the centre for trade with Europe and further afield. The streets were built on a grid pattern, which suggests there were laws controlling building work. Surrounding the town was a high defensive earth wall topped by a wooden **PALISADE**.

People came to trade goods and crafts, and many set up small workshops for pottery, leatherwork and weaving. As the barter system gave way to a coin-based commerce the Vikings built a mint.

London had been a substantial Roman city. It stood at the meeting point of several Saxon kingdoms, and developed as a place for trade. The River Thames made it easy to transport goods. London became the seat of kings and a focus for wars. The Vikings attacked it several times:

"…with three hundred and fifty ships to the mouth of the river Thames, and sacked … the city of London, which lies on the north bank of the river Thames."

Source – The Life of King Alfred, by Asser, Bishop of Sherborne, 893 AD

Towns Glossary

administrative	Relating to organisation	**habitable**	Fit to live in
afield	Far away	**haven**	Safe place
burh	Defensive market town	**mint**	A place where money is made
commerce	Business or trade	**mouth**	The part of a river where it meets the sea
garrison	Place where soldiers are based	**palisade**	Fence

See also: Saxons and Vikings 4–5; Administration 8–9; Language 22–23; Sports and Pastimes 30–31

CASE STUDY

Burhs

Planned by Alfred the Great, burhs were the first 'national' defence system. Each could accommodate people from the surrounding countryside during enemy raids. They were located mainly along the **BORDER** with the Danelaw, and were usually on high ground surrounded by a wall and a ditch.

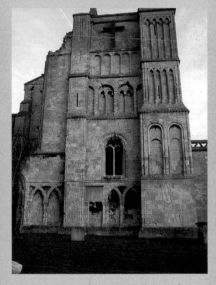

Malmesbury Abbey in the Saxon burh of Malmesbury.

Malmesbury, in Wiltshire, is one of the oldest Saxon burhs, and survives as a market town famous for its Saxon abbey. The position and aspect of the town was described eloquently by the historian John Leland:

"The toun of Malmesbyri stondith on the very toppe of a greate slaty rok, and ys wonderfully defended by nature."

Source – description of Malmesbury by the 16th-century historian John Leland

Architecture and Art

The materials used for houses and other buildings depended very much on what was available locally. Most Saxon homes were constructed from a wooden frame and had walls of **WATTLE AND DAUB**. Where more money was available, to build churches, monasteries and other important buildings, stone was used. Early Saxon churches were generally small and it was only later in the period that **AISLES** or towers were added. Vikings also used timber and other readily-available materials for building.

HOMES AND CHURCHES

There are few examples of Saxon **BUILDINGS** in England. Most were made from wood and have not survived. Only buildings like monasteries, churches and other grand buildings were made of more-durable stone. In his Life of King Alfred the chronicler Asser describes construction on a grand scale:

"Of the royal halls and chambers, wonderfully built of stone and of wood at his command? Of royal vills made of masonry removed from the old sites and most admirably rebuilt in more suitable places by the king's order."

St Mary's in Breamore, Hampshire, is one of the few surviving Saxon churches, and was probably built about 1000 AD.

Many Saxon churches were destroyed during the reign of Henry VIII. A few buildings remain, though many have later additions or have been incorporated into larger buildings.

Early Saxon churches had a simple layout, usually just a long rectangular shape that ran east to west. This developed in later Saxon times to the shape of a cross. The inside of the church was plain except for a few carved stone panels and pilaster strips, long strips of stone that formed a simple criss-cross pattern.

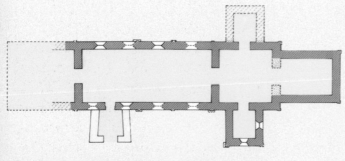

This plan shows the typical layout of a Saxon church.

Source – The Life of King Alfred, by Asser, Bishop of Sherborne, 893 AD

SAXON BUILDINGS

A reconstructed Saxon settlement at West Stow, Suffolk.

Like the Vikings, Saxons built their houses mainly from wood. A wooden **FRAME** would be clad using planks of wood, or sometimes with wattle and daub. Roofs were usually thatched. The homes of ordinary people were simple and small. They usually had just one room where everyone ate and slept, and were built in small settlements. You can visit **RECONSTRUCTED** Saxon villages such as the one at West Stow in Suffolk.

Wealthy Saxons had larger houses with several rooms. The house of a wealthy trader or chief would be richly decorated, with designs or pictures on the walls, as described by the writer of *Beowulf*:

"... And he resolved to build a hall, a large and noble feasting-hall of whose splendours men would always speak ... Then I heard that tribes without number, were given orders to decorate the hall."

> Source – Beowulf, written down about 1000 AD

Architecture and Art Glossary

anchorite	Person living in a monastery	**incorporated**	Made a part of something larger
clad	Covered		
daub	Sticky plaster	**thatched**	A roof of straw
gild	Cover with a thin layer of precious metal	**unalloyed**	Pure
		vill	Estate
illuminated	Decorated with gold and silver	**wattle**	Woven twigs used for building

See also: Viking Raids 6–7; Society 12–13; Economy 14–15; Towns 24–25; Family and Marriage 18–19

CASE STUDY

An illustrated page from the Linisfarne Gospels. This page shows the introduction to St. John's Gospel.

Art and craft

Viking crafts were usually practical, such as the elaborate brooches used by women to secure their dresses, intricate grave carvings or beautiful pots for storing food. They often depict animals and other creatures in linked patterns.

This style was also common in Christian Saxon art, as can be seen in the illuminated pages of the Lindisfarne Gospels. The Gospels are masterpieces of book production, and many hours of painstaking work went into writing and illustrating them by hand as mechanical printing had not been invented. This is a description of the book being made:

"AEthelwald, Bishop of the Lindisfarne islanders, bound it on the outside and covered it, as he knew well how to do. And Billfrith, the anchorite, wrought the ornaments on the outside and adorned it with gold and with gems and gilded silver, unalloyed metal..."

> Source – The Anglo-Saxon Chronicle, written 9th–12th century

Law and Justice

Saxon kings were responsible for maintaining law and order. The king made new laws with the help of the Witan (a body of wise men or counsellors). There were no prisons, and people were often punished with a FINE. For some CRIMES, a nose or a hand could be cut off. If a person hurt or killed someone, he had to pay money, known as 'wergild', to the victim's relatives. To prove that he was not guilty the ACCUSED had to find people to swear an OATH of his innocence. If he failed to do so, he might be sent for trial by ORDEAL.

TAKING OATH

The basic principle of the law in Saxon times still exists today, in that an accused person is presumed to be innocent until guilt can be proved. Anyone who denied an accusation of wrongdoing had the right to prove his innocence.

The **DEFENDANT** would swear an oath, and find others who would also swear to his innocence. The oath of a more important person, like a thegn, carried greater weight than that of a lower-class person like a ceorl.

Under the law of King Alfred, a defendant would swear with the words:

"By the Lord, I am guiltless, both in deed and counsel, and of the charge of which [person's name] *accuses me."*

Usually this and any other oaths were enough to clear the accused person. Though it might seem that this system could be open to abuse, it was not the case in practice. The areas in

Swearing an oath in court was taken very seriously by the Vikings and Saxons.

which **COURTS** were held were small and everyone knew each other. A person who was known to be guilty would find it difficult to persuade others to support him. Those involved in administering local justice also knew the people involved, as well as local opinion. This is why, very often, no other evidence was given.

Sometimes, a defendant was not considered honest enough to take an oath, so was allowed to put forward a witnesses, who would swear:

"In the name of Almighty God, ... I saw with my eyes and heard with ears that which I pronounce with him."

Source – *The Laws of Alfred, Guthrum, and Edward the Elder, c.10th Century*

Words to use in your project

admission (confession)	
district (area)	
judiciary (body of judges)	
proof (evidence that establishes the truth)	
statute (law)	
testimony (written or spoken statement)	

TRIAL BY ORDEAL

Ordeals were carried out in Saxon and Viking times to judge whether people were guilty or innocent of certain crimes.

Trial by ordeal was used only if a defendant insisted he was innocent and could not find others to support him. The church undertook to administer the ordeal. Time was allowed for religious fasting and for the defendant to change his mind and confess. If he still protested innocence, he usually had to decide between ordeal by water or iron.

For one ordeal by water, the accused was thrown into a river or pond. If he floated he was judged guilty, and if he sank he was innocent. Other ordeals involved boiling water or bars of hot iron. If the defendant's wounds festered, he was judged guilty (and often died). This is an extract of one of the rules relating to trial by ordeal:

"And concerning the ordeal we enjoin by command of God, and of the archbishop, and of all the bishops: that no man come within the church after the fire is borne in with which the ordeal shall be heated, except the mass-priest, and him who shall go thereto..."

Source – The Laws of King Athelstan 924-939 AD

Law and Justice Glossary

accuse	Bring formal charges against
borne	Carried
confess	Admit a fault or crime
counsel	To give advice
defendant	A person accused in a court of law
fasting	Period without eating
mass-priest	The priest who says Mass
ordeal	Method of trial in which the accused was exposed to physical danger
swear	Make a declaration by an appeal to something sacred

CASE STUDY

Fines were imposed for many crimes in Saxon England.

Laws in the hundreds

As Saxon England became unified, laws governing the whole land were passed. Systems were put in place to make sure they were observed, determine whether they had been broken, and decide appropriate punishment.

The king and the witan (senior council) considered issues and agreed laws. Eolderman and thegns made sure they were applied in their area. If the outcome of a local trial was disputed, it could be taken higher, perhaps to a hundred court (a 'hundred' was a large area), which met frequently.

In early Saxon times, punishments (usually fines) were set out, like these from 6th-century Kent:

"If a shoulder be lamed, let bot [payment] be made with thirty shillings. If an ear be struck off, let bot be made with twelve shillings. Let him who breaks the chin-bone pay for it with twenty shillings."

Source – The Laws of King AEthelberht, 560–616 AD

See also: Religion 10–11; Family and Marriage 18–19; Wars and Weapons 20–21; Sports and Pastimes 30–31

Sports and Pastimes

Most people had some time to play GAMES, take part in tests of skill or enjoy general entertainment. Most of the games played challenged either the physical or mental strengths of the participants. BETTING on their outcome was also popular. Music, poetry, storytelling and solving riddles were also popular pastimes. Fairs and market gatherings were often places where people took part in these activities, but they also liked playing games like chess or listening to tales and poetry at home.

GAMES THEY PLAYED

Tests of physical **STRENGTH** such as wrestling and weightlifting were popular. Wrestling could be between individuals or teams, and simply involved trying to get an opponent off his feet. It was usually very rough, however, and contestants often ended up with broken bones.

Ball games rather like hockey, hurling or shinty were also played. Juggling was popular both as a test of skill and for entertainment. Richer people enjoyed pastimes including falconry and bear-baiting.

BOARD GAMES were very popular during the Saxon and Viking period. The word tafl (literally 'table') was used to describe a board game, with the pieces being referred to as toflur or hunn. Very early chess pieccs found on the Scottish Isle of Lewis are believed to be of 10th-century Viking origin. Other games including backgammon were also played. Chess pieces, counters and dice could be made from wood, bone, antlers or even walrus tusks. Five stones was a game like the modern Jacks, and Nine Men's Morris was similar to draughts.

Other sports involved animals, including bear-baiting. This extract from Sverri's Saga seems to involve performing dogs:

"Two players... who made small dogs jump over high poles in front of high born men, and the more high born they were the higher they jumped."

Board games were very popular with Vikings, since many games of skill were based on the themes of war or capture.

Source – Sverri's Saga, c.1200

Words to use in your project	competition (sporting activity) oral (spoken) participate (take part)	puzzle (a game to test knowledge) recreation (entertainment)	restriction (limit) sprint (run at full speed)

MUSIC AND STORYTELLING

A favourite pastime of the period was music and **STORYTELLING**. Vikings enjoyed sitting together listening to tales of their gods and other heroic events. Not many people could write, so the only way of preserving their heritage was to tell these stories for others to hear and remember. Stories of ancient heroes were very popular and to recite it a scop (poet and storyteller) had to remember lines of verse. Scops would perform for kings and rich people as is in the 7th-century poem *Widsith*:

"When Scilling [Widsith's harp] and I, with a clear voice, raised the song before our royal lord, loud with the harp I sounded the melody."

Popular musical instruments of Viking times included whistles made of bone and wooden panpipes.

Singing and music were also enjoyed and there were professional musicians, called 'gleemen' who played at feasts and other special occasions. People played a range of instruments including harps, lyres, and whistles, and dancing was also very popular.

Source – Widsith, an Anglo-Saxon poem, c. 7th century

Sports and Pastimes Glossary

bear-baiting	Sport in which a bear is attacked by many dogs	**panpipes**	Musical instrument played by blowing across a row of pipes
falconry	Using a trained bird of prey to catch birds or small animals	**pastime**	Way of spending spare time
		recite	Speak aloud
juggle	Perform tricks using balls or other items	**smith**	Person who makes or repairs metal objects
lyre	Small instrument like a harp	**verse**	Poetry

See also: Viking Raids 6–7; Food and Drink 16–17; Family and Marriage 18–19; Law and Justice 28–29

CASE STUDY

Riddle-me-ree

One game played during Saxon times was riddling, or trying to guess the answer of a word puzzle. Many **RIDDLES** had double meanings, and were often in rhyme. A riddle could be anything from one to a hundred lines. This is a popular Saxon riddle:

"I'm by nature solitary, scarred by spear and wounded by sword, weary of battle. I frequently see the face of war, and fight hateful enemies; yet I hold no hope of help being brought to me in the battle, before I'm eventually done to death. In the stronghold of the city sharp-edged swords, skillfully forged in the flame by smiths bite deeply into me. I can but await a more fearsome encounter; it is not for me to discover in the city any of those doctors who heal grievous wounds with roots and herbs. The scars from sword wounds gape wider and wider death blows are dealt me by day and by night."

Source – Exeter Book, 1070 AD
Answer: a shield

Index

SAXON TIMELINE

793 AD
Vikings attack the monastery at Lindisfarne (Holy Island).

865 AD
Vikings fight as one large army of Danes.

871 AD
King Ethelred killed at the Battle of Ashdown. Alfred becomes king.

878 AD
Alfred defeats the Danes at the battle of Edington.

886 AD
England divided into the Viking-ruled Danelaw in the north, while Alfred rules the south.

893 AD
Asser, the Bishop of Sherborne writes The Life of King Alfred.

899 AD
Ethelred The Unready becomes king.

1013 AD
Sweyn overthrows Ethelred, but dies the following year.

1016 AD.
Canute crowned king, and rules over a large, prosperous empire.

1042 AD
Edward the Confessor becomes king.

1065 AD
Edward dies and Harold is named king.

October 1066 AD
Harold defeated at the Battle of Hastings. William, Duke of Normandy, becomes king.

PICTURE CREDITS: Ancient Art Library: 4-5 all, 8-9 all, 10b, 11c, 21 all, 22-23 all, 24-25 all, 28b, 31c. Corbis: 13 all, 14-15 all, 29br, 29t. Mary Evans: 6-7 all, 12b, 26b, 27 all, 18b, 19c, 20b, Jorvik Viking Centre: 31c.